For Jack
on the occasion of your
Uncle Michael's 60th birthday
June 25, 2009
He loved Seaside so!
Love, Uncle Kal

We dedicate this project to all who've been touched by the
magic of this place

AT THE WATER'S EDGE

The MAGIC of ASTORIA, SEASIDE & CANNON BEACH

ADAM CARLSEN & DONALD MASTERSON

oceanrider

INTRODUCTION

"The jewel of the Pacific", "the beach of a thousand wonders", "the northwest's most popular ocean resort", "a magnificent coastal wilderness"; these phrases have all been used to describe a stretch of the Pacific coast from historic Astoria at the mouth of the Columbia River, to scenic, touristy Seaside fifteen miles south, and on to artsy Cannon Beach a bit further down Highway 101.

Set like an artist's finest work in a geographic frame of the mighty Columbia River to the north, the Pacific Ocean to the west, and Neahkahnie Mountain to the south; this 30 mile stretch of the Oregon Coast has been drawing visitors from the Northwest and beyond for decades.

With I-5 connecting to Highway 30 from the north and easy access from the Willamette Valley over Highway 26, Cannon Beach, Seaside and Astoria have evolved into some of the most desired destinations on the Pacific coast. Although these three communities are similar regionally and geographically, they have each developed independently and maintain a certain unique identity that separates, yet connects them in some way today.

As long-time residents of the area, many elements of this section of the Oregon coast have always intrigued us. Paramount in our minds is the physical beauty and peaceful serenity of the area; but also fascinating is the common thread that binds three very different, yet closely related coastal communities. In recent years, it has become more common for visitors to include each community as a destination on their itinerary; perhaps to experience a diversity of location and feel, or maybe just to visit a favorite restaurant, aquarium, or museum.

It seems that Cannon Beach, Seaside and Astoria are drawing closer as the years pass; like acquaintances suddenly discovering they have more in common than before. While Seaside has historically been the premier tourist locale, it took a bit longer for Cannon Beach to be discovered, and Astoria is even now discovering its new identity as a treasured place to visit.

We hope to capture through this book the common thread that binds these three communities; places that sit "At the Water's Edge" on Oregon's Pacific Coast. It is here where geographic beauty and uniqueness flow together like the water that surrounds us, to provide a place to visit that you will cherish always.

D. Masterson

G. Vetter   D. Masterson

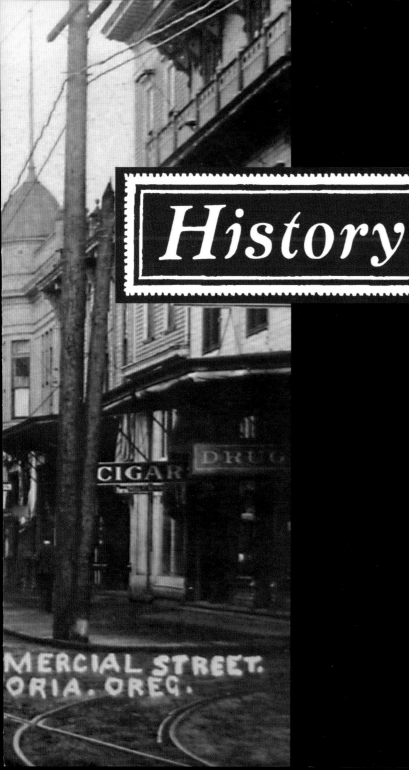

History

IN 1835, JOHN JACOB ASTOR APPROACHED writer Washington Irving about writing a novel highlighting Astoria's early history and the importance of Astor's Pacific Fur Company to the region. Had Irving continued to chronicle Astoria's history in the years following, such a novel would have read at times like a tragedy - at times a glorious epic. The city has had to reinvent itself through the years in structure and identity. For many years, Astoria was one of the most important economic hubs in the Pacific Northwest. Twice, it literally rose from the ashes of massive fires that decimated large portions of downtown. The fishing and timber industries, on which the economy was built, fell on hard times in the latter part of the century and Astoria once again had to overcome adversity. Such a rich history of achievements, challenges, and tragedies has created the unique and resilient community of today.

CAPTAIN ROBERT GRAY
is greeted by the natives at the
mouth of the Columbia River in 1792

A SHORT HISTORY of ASTORIA

Astoria's history began with two prominent American expeditions of exploration: Lewis and Clarks' historic journey across the country and the fur trading exploits of Captain Robert Gray. Prior to Lewis and Clark's historic encounter with the area, explorer Robert Gray and crew arrived at the mouth of the Columbia River in 1792. Their journey was actually an economic one. Gray was sailing the Pacific Northwest in search of furs to trade. The journey into the mouth of the Columbia was his second visit to the region. Initial attempts to navigate the treacherous sandbars at the entrance to the river were unsuccessful. Gray finally ordered a small sail-boat to enter and map out a safe route. On May 17, 1792 his ship the Columbia finally made safe passage into the mighty Columbia River. They spent nine full days in the river, trading with the natives and storing fresh water. Gray subsequently made American claims to the river and named it Columbia after his faithful sailing ship.

Captain Robert Gray Mural Courtesy of Oregon State Capitol, Legislative Administration Committee

LEWIS and CLARK

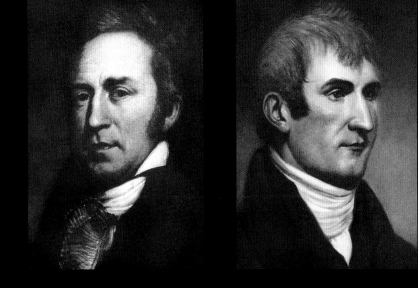

In 1805, the Lewis and Clark Expedition arrived in the Astoria area from down the Columbia River. They built a log-structured encampment southwest of Astoria, along the banks of the Lewis and Clark River and called it Fort Clatsop. The fort stands today as a national monument, visited each year by thousands of people. The area surrounding Astoria was home to the Clatsop Indians, many of whom lived in villages along the mouth of the river. During their time at Fort Clatsop, the expedition traded extensively with the Clatsops. Following a wet, miserable winter, they set out east again towards home, bringing with them tales of abundant otter and beaver in the mysterious west.

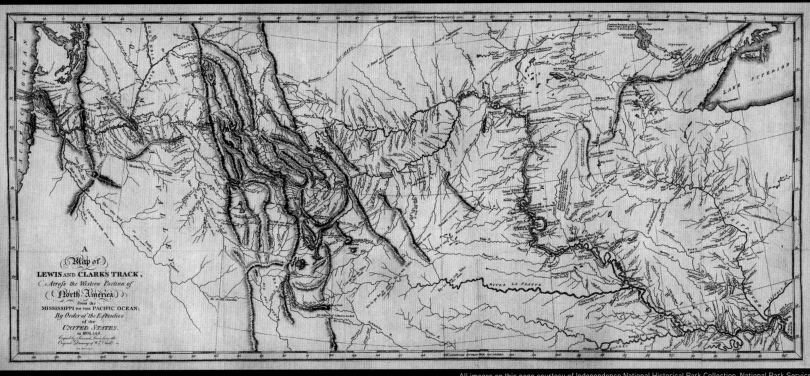

THE FIRST SETTLERS

In 1810, John Jacob Astor, a businessman and fur trader from the east coast, sent agents out west from his Pacific Fur Company, to create a trading post along the river. This outpost was the center of the company's northwest trading. Astoria's agents established Fort Astoria in 1811, the first permanent United States settlement west of the Rocky Mountains. John Jacob Astor's dreams of wealth in the west would come to an end when the company failed and was subsequently sold to the British in 1813.

American Missionaries and adventurous pioneers following the Oregon Trail began trickling into Astoria in the 1830's and 1840's. As the Oregon territory grew in population, so did the population and commerce of Astoria. It would become an important port city, with close access to the ocean through the mouth of the Columbia River. In 1847, the first post office west of the Rocky Mountains was established in the home of local resident John M. Shively. Fueled by the rich growth of timber surrounding Astoria and its port status, sawmills and logging camps sprang to life in the next few decades.

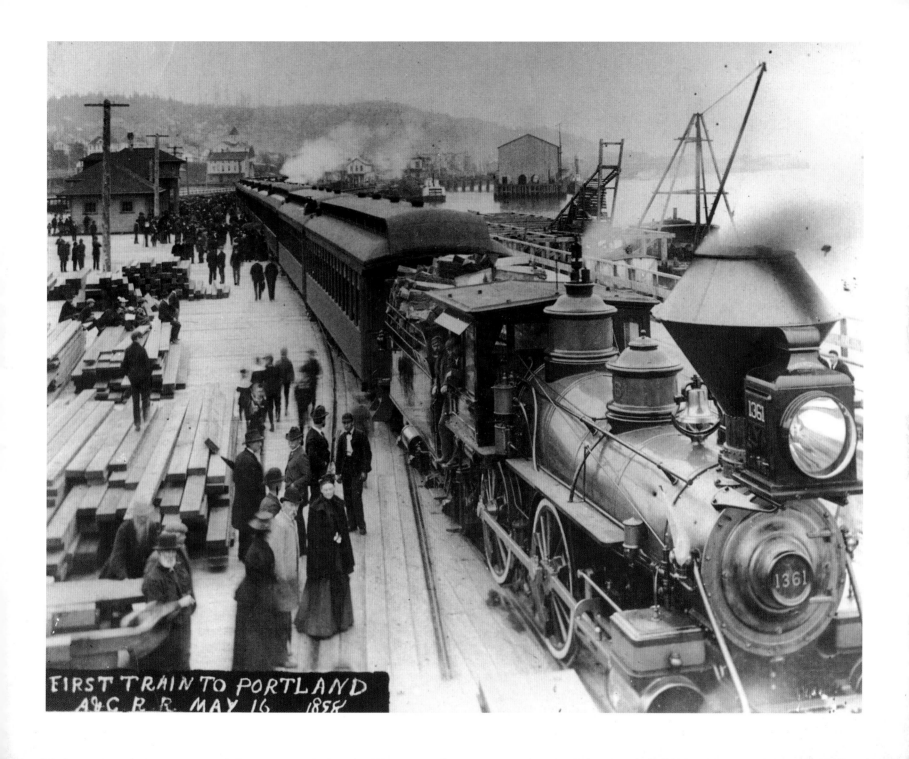

FIRST TRAIN TO PORTLAND
A&C R.R. MAY 16 1898

Salmon abounded in the Columbia River and the fishing industry soon took root. These industries brought a large influx of settlers from Finland, Norway, and Sweden. Chinese settlers also arrived, to work in the many canneries in the area. Astoria thrived in the latter part of the 1800's, and Victorian-style homes were constructed lining the hills of the city. Many of these homes still stand today and their presence above the Columbia River is a highlight of any visit to Astoria. As a result of this exponential growth, Astoria was officially incorporated in 1876.

With settlement, came children and the natural need for an educational system. Before 1854, residents taught their children in the home. The first school district, No. 1, was established in 1854. Classes were held in a local Methodist Church, until Astoria's first school building was constructed in 1859, fueled by the growth of the fishing and logging industries, the population continued to expand and the need for schools followed this trend. The first Catholic school, Holy Names Academy for Young Ladies, opened in 1846. It was destroyed by fire in 1923, but was rebuilt as the Star of the Sea School on October 20, 1924. The first public High School was opened in 1911, followed by the Astoria Elementary and Robert Gray Elementary schools in 1925.

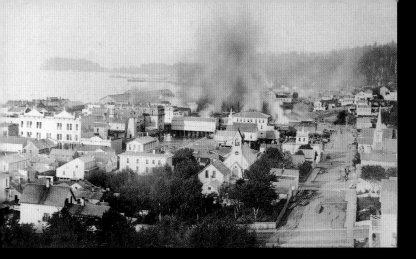

Astoria's history has twice been marred by tragedy in the form of fire. In 1883, a fire began at the Clatsop Mill and spread quickly through the local business district. Again, in 1922, a larger fire nearly wiped out the entire downtown area and business district. It raced, unstopped block-by-block, through the basements of buildings connected together by wooden via-ducts. An attempt was even made to dynamite part of downtown to stop the fire. Within a span of only twenty-four hours, thirty-two city blocks downtown had been destroyed and 2,500 people were left homeless. The city was able to rise from the ashes of both tragedies, rebuild the economy, and move towards the future.

Sadly, the strength of Astoria's economy, built on the backbone of fishing, logging, and fish processing began to steadily decline in the 1960's and 1970's. Brisk business in ports upriver at Portland and beyond, directly affected Astoria's industry and economy. Approximately 30 canneries were present along this section of the Columbia River in 1945. Bumblebee Seafood relocated its Astoria headquarters in 1970, and eventually closed its last cannery in 1980. The logging economy faltered as well, culminated by the closing of the Astoria Plywood Mill in 1989. At the time of the closing, it was the city's largest employer. Finally, all railroad service to Astoria was officially discontinued in 1996.

Following the economic hardships Astoria sustained in the later part of the 1900's, the city began to reinvent itself in unique and interesting ways. It is now a major tourist destination on the Pacific Coast. The downtown, which for much of the last twenty years reflected the city's declining economy, is now beginning to show healthy signs of life; with new storefronts, funky restaurants, galleries, theaters and more. Each year, cruise ships dock in the river and flood the town with hundreds of new visitors. Astoria's rich history, Scandinavian heritage, Lewis and Clark legacy, and breath-taking location, are just a few of the many characteristics that bring people this city by the river.

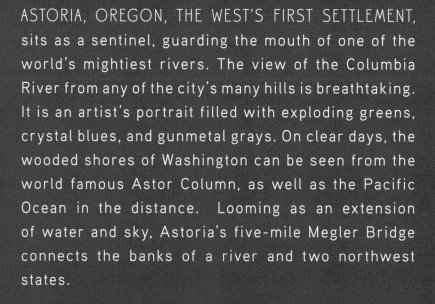

Art & Atmosphere

ASTORIA, OREGON, THE WEST'S FIRST SETTLEMENT, sits as a sentinel, guarding the mouth of one of the world's mightiest rivers. The view of the Columbia River from any of the city's many hills is breathtaking. It is an artist's portrait filled with exploding greens, crystal blues, and gunmetal grays. On clear days, the wooded shores of Washington can be seen from the world famous Astor Column, as well as the Pacific Ocean in the distance. Looming as an extension of water and sky, Astoria's five-mile Megler Bridge connects the banks of a river and two northwest states.

The city's location and geography have for years inspired artists and photographers, all seeking through their own medium, to capture its beauty. On a canvas, in a story, or through a camera's lens, the art and atmosphere is reflected in these pages. Enjoy Astoria through the eyes and perspectives of those artisans who have captured and loved its unique character and beauty.

N. Thomas

Noel Thomas aws

G. Vetter

D. Frank

C. Bryant

T. Robinson

23

D. Masterson

ASTORIA: A CHANGING IDENTITY

A modern snapshot down any community's main street is a frozen picture that tells a story. The light on the buildings in that moment, or the people and vehicles stopped in time give an instant impression of identity and life. Stand today and look down Astoria's main street, and you will see a town redefining itself. Take a picture if you'd like, but understand that there is more to Astoria than the one moment you capture. The progression of history and events too numerous to recount, have shaped the present identity of a diverse and interesting Columbia River community.

D. Masterson

D. Frank

Astoria began as the oldest settlement in Pacific Northwest region when John Jacob Astor established a fur-trading post in 1815 at the mouth of the Columbia River. It would soon become a thriving port-town, even surviving two wide-spread and devastating fires in 1883 and 1922. Famous American writer Washington Irving wrote a novel simply entitled, "Astoria" in 1835 to commemorate Astoria's early history and importance to the Northwest region. The economy was later built around industries such as logging, milling, fishing and canning. For many years, this economy and culture defined the community as a less than genteel place to live or visit.

In the 1960's and 1970's, these industries failed and Astoria was again faced with the prospect of change. Blessed with a spectacular location, classic architecture and flair, and an abundance of natural beauty; it seemed only natural that its evolution as a visitor destination would begin. Observable change since that time has been gradual. Completed renovation of Astoria's historic Liberty theatre in 2002 is a perfect representation of the community's overall direction.

Astoria today, viewed down main-street, has a unique look and feel, created by a blending of the old and new. Art galleries, hip cafes, classy restaurants, shops, and hotels line the streets. Above them, many of the town's Victorian homes are being restored to their original shine. Gone is the feel of a crumbling, blue-collar port-town, and in its place is a new identity with a direct sense of purpose. For Astoria, a community rich in history and personality, the future is open to any number of opportunities.

"Touch of Astoria (Fall)" Bill W. Dodge

MERWYN
HOTEL
ASTORIA

EMPLOYEE PARKING
ONLY
UNAUTHORIZED VEHICLES WILL BE TOWED
AWAY AT OWNERS EXPENSE.

OFFICE

NORWEGIAN SUN
NASSAU

UOMI HALL
FINNISH BROTHERHOOD

EST. 1886

C. Meyer

D. Masterson

M. Mathers Courtesy of Columbia River Maritime Museum

M. Larson

N. Thomas

ASTORIA EVENTS

The history of Astoria is a rich tale of a community constantly overcoming the odds to reinvent itself time and again. What began as an economy built on fishing, logging, milling and canning, has today become an attractive destination for visitors to this part of the Pacific coast.

For many coastal communities, the planned event has become a crucial piece in the overall goal to bring as many visitors as possible. These events often highlight the uniqueness of an area - its personality, history or even potential future identity. Astoria hosts a series of events throughout the year, catering to both visitors and area residents.

The Fisher Poets gathering in February is perhaps the most iconic and sentimental Astoria event; tapping into the fading remnants of an industry centered on commercial fishing and the emotions of a still significant sub-culture. Spend a weekend listening to the poetry and writing of fishermen, fisherwomen, and many others who have called the sea their home. Writing events and seminars focusing on the craft and taught by local practitioners take place throughout the weekend.

During the last full weekend in April, The Crab and Seafood Festival at the Clatsop County Fairgrounds highlights the regions' best offerings, with nearly 150 food and drink booths. Each year, approximately 20,000 people visit this event for a weekend filled with fun, live entertainment, wine tasting, and the best local seafood. A highlight of the event is the Astoria Rotary Club's famous crab dinner. During the festival, numerous Oregon wineries display their best offerings, regional artisans exhibit their work and, handcrafted beers from around the state are served at the event's beer garden.

D. Beeston

D. Masterson

D. Masterson

Astoria Chamber of Commerce

D. Beeston

Summertime brings the Scandinavian Festival in June and the Clatsop County Fair in August. The Festival celebrates Astoria's rich Scandinavian history with traditional costumes, folk dancing, music, and booths featuring a variety of delicacies. Other events include the crowning of Miss Scandinavia, a torchlight parade, the Optog Parade, Midsummer pole rising and Hex-Burning bonfire. The Clatsop County Fair is an Astoria tradition dating back to 1905. Attendees enjoy farm animal displays and demonstrations, food options, and a carnival.

Each of these events is a celebration of the rich history, geography, seasons and culture of Astoria. They serve to bring the community together, entertain visitors and ultimately create a welcoming atmosphere for many to enjoy.

D. Frank

M. Vargas

ASTORIA CUISINE

Through its years of changing and developing identity, from canneries and fishing docks, to its current reinvention as a funky, upbeat naturalistic haven for tourists and locals alike, Astoria has also seen an influx of quality dining options. Though not historically known for its restaurant scene, in recent years the number of quality cafes, fine dining restaurants, family eateries, coffee shops, and bakeries has increased dramatically. It is an interesting mix of the old and the new, the "greasy spoon" and the upscale.

The community's rich history of seafood harvesting remains relevant and influential today, as most restaurants feature fresh fish on their menus and a variety of bounties from the sea. Much of the character and diversity of Astoria's dining scene is not dissimilar to a university town, boasting funky coffee and sandwich shops, "hole in the wall" cafes, and organic bakeries.

BAKED ALASKA, located on the waterfront with stunning views of the Columbia River, features a menu built on the Northwest's finest seafood offerings. Chef Christopher Holen and his wife, Jennifer, began the business as a mobile soup kitchen serving sourdough bread bowls and soup in Alaska. In August of 2000, they opened a permanent, seven-table café in downtown Astoria. Baked Alaska was then expanded in the spring of 2001 to its current, location on the Columbia River. Serving lunch and dinner, the expansive menu features starters, seafood pastas, salads, a variety of fish entrees, steaks, delectable desserts and more. Enjoy also a drink from the full service lounge. Baked Alaska is truly one of the northwest's finest.

BROILED PACIFIC SEA SCALLOPS

Serves 1

INGREDIENTS

Clarified butter

1 tsp. minced ginger

1 oz. shaved fennel

1/2 tsp. minced garlic

2 oz. apple-cider vinegar

4 oz. white wine

1/4 of a Fuji apple, sliced

1/2 cup heavy cream

1 tbsp. whole butter

Salt and pepper to taste

METHOD

Scallops (3): Lightly drizzle with clarified butter, season with salt and pepper and broil until semi-firm and golden. Sauce (pan sauce): Heat sauté pan over medium high heat, coat bottom of pan with clarified butter. Sauté ingredients beginning with ginger, then add fennel and garlic. Be careful not to burn the garlic. Deglaze with apple-cider vinegar, then add white wine and reduce by half. Swirl in heavy cream and apples and reduce by 1/3. Remove sauce from heat, swirl in cold butter and season to taste. Cook 4 oz. fresh pasta al dente, then strain. Toss with extra virgin olive oil, salt and pepper. Pour sauce over pasta, top with scallops and garnish with fennel frond.

*Serve with a Fennel, Apple and Ginger Sauce over Fresh Black Pepper Linguini

D. Masterson

D. Masterson

THUNDERMUCK TUNA

Serves 1

Coffee dusted albacore tuna with a honey, ginger sesame sauce and balsamic vinegar reduction. Served with Chinese black rice and baby carrots.

INGREDIENTS

Tuna

4 - 5 oz. center cut albacore tuna steak

Fresh ground coffee

Salt

Pepper

Sauce

1 tsp. minced ginger

3 tbsp. honey

1 tbsp. sesame oil

1 tbsp. rice wine vinegar

Pinch of toasted sesame seeds

1/2 tsp. dry mustard

METHOD

Dust tuna steak in fresh ground coffee and lightly season with salt and pepper. Heat sauté pan over medium high heat and coat with sesame oil. Sear each side of tuna ever so slightly. Remove tuna from pan and thinly slice. Whisk together and drizzle sauce over sliced tuna. Garnish plate with balsamic vinegar reduction.

VANILLA CHEESCAKE WITH A WALNUT CRUST

Serves 6

INGREDIENTS

Crust:

3 cups walnuts

1/3 cup brown sugar

4 tbsp. butter

Cheesecake:

2 1/2 pds. of cream cheese, softened

1 1/2 cup sugar

3 eggs

2 1/2 tsp. vanilla extract

METHOD

Crust: Blend ingredients together in a food processor, chopped up, but not too fine. Lightly coat the interior of a 10" spring form pan with cold butter. Put the crust mixture in the pan and evenly spread on the bottom and up the sides to evenly cover the pan. Bake at 350 degrees for 20 minutes.

D. Masterson

Cheesecake: Beat cream cheese using the paddle at high speed in an electric mixture until it is light and fluffy. Gradually add the sugar, beating well. Add eggs one at a time, beating well after each addition. Add in vanilla last. Pour in to walnut crust. Bake at 350 degrees for 40 minutes. Turn oven off and open door slightly. Leave cheesecake in oven for an additional 30 minutes. Remove from oven and allow cooling in a draft free place. Cover and refrigerate for 8 hours before serving. Garnish with fresh kiwi and blueberry sauce.

S. Goodnough Courtesy of Union Fishermen's Co-operative Packing Co.

R. Hurley

J. Hull

D. Masterson

T. Robinson

D. Orange

N. Thomas

R. Hurley

R. Hurley

FORT CLATSOP

In the winter of 1805 – 1806, the Lewis and Clark Expedition, exhausted and nearing the end of a long journey across the country, established a permanent settlement just southwest of Astoria. Fort Clatsop, named after the local Clatsop Indian tribe, was built alongside the Lewis and Clark River as the last encampment before the expedition would return home to St. Louis, Missouri. Using the fort as home-base of sorts, they explored the area further, traveling to the Seaside area to build the famous salt-cairn. They also made their way over Tillamook head to Cannon Beach in search of a beached whale, hoping to procure much needed whale blubber and oil. The fort was left behind when, after three months of residence, Lewis and Clark and the expedition returned home.

A replica of Fort Clatsop was built in 1955 to celebrate the sesquicentennial celebration of the expedition's remarkable journey of discovery. It is now protected as a State and National Park. Over the years, the fort has hosted thousands of people within its log-built walls. A gift shop, museum, and information center, run by a friendly and helpful staff, educates and welcomes interested visitors.

A fire destroyed the original replica in 2005. Fort Clatsop - the memorial of a remarkable journey, a reminder of America's first pioneers, and a place for visitors to connect with our country's history; rose from the ashes the next year, rebuilt by a group of selfless volunteers. It stands today as an icon, the legacy of a courageous group of explorers and the indomitable spirit that our country was built on.

FORT CLATSOP
NATIONAL MEMORIAL

D. Masterson

M. Larson

© National Park Service

R. Hurley

N. Thomas

R. Hurley

D. Beeston

D. Frank

K. Nyberg

D. Masterson

D. Masterson

Vargas/ Masterson

D. Masterson

D. Masterson

HOLLYWOOD COMES TO TOWN

Astoria, Oregon, the first permanent Pacific coast settlement is a town surrounded by staggering geographic beauty. It is blessed with the majestic Columbia River, and a profusion of forests, hills and rivers nearby. Its unique history has also been maintained, with Victorian homes, a classic downtown corridor, and steep San Francisco-like hills. It is little wonder then, with such an abundance of local flair and natural beauty that Hollywood has been drawn to the area for filming projects.

It began with the classic hit, "The Goonies" in 1984; an adventure story where a group of young friends discover a pirate's treasure map in the attic of their house. The map leads them through underground caverns, past booby traps and skeletons, into the path of bumbling crooks, and ultimately to an ancient pirates ship full of treasure. "The Goonies" house is still visited regularly by the film's legion of fans.

The family drama "Short Circuit" was released in 1986 and also features one of Astoria's turn-of-the-century homes. Three years later, the film "Come See the Paradise" was filmed in the community. "Kindergarten Cop", completed in 1990, is along with "The Goonies" Astoria's most famous Hollywood production. Local filming locations included The Bayview Motel, The Red Lion Hotel, Astor Elementary School, and a Victorian home at 414 Exchange St. Community icons such as the Astoria-Megler Bridge and the Astor column are also shown in the film. Two popular films, "The Teenage Mutant Ninja Turtles" and "Free Willy" were filmed in the early 1990's in and around Astoria. Keiko, the famous Oregon Coast Orca Whale starred as Willy in the latter film.

As Astoria continues to grow into a premier visitor destination, with a fine balance of the old and new; there is little doubt that Hollywood will come to town again very soon. Hang around town often enough and you may just get to be an extra someday!

D. Masterson

D. Masterson

M. Vargas

D. Masterson

SEASIDE

The Turn-around - Seaside - Ore

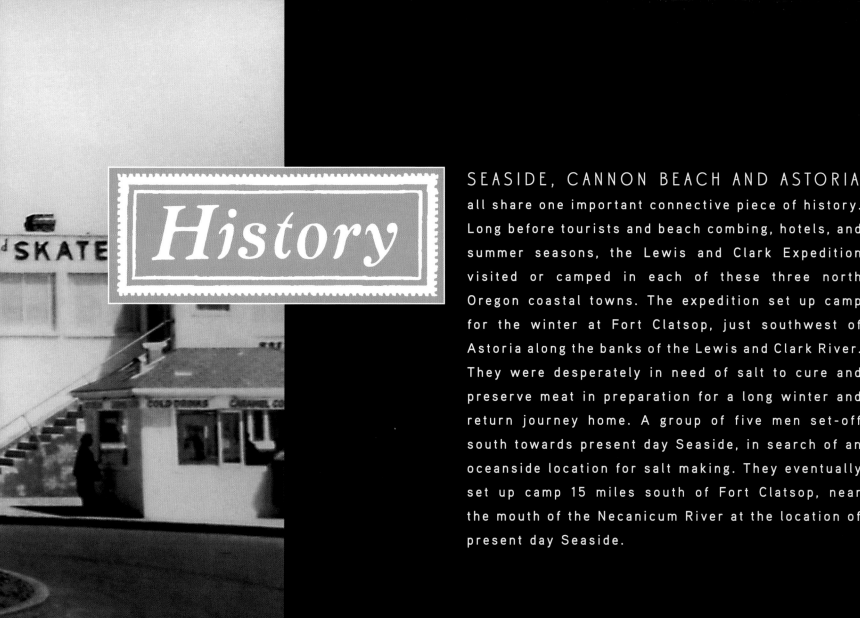

History

SEASIDE, CANNON BEACH AND ASTORIA all share one important connective piece of history. Long before tourists and beach combing, hotels, and summer seasons, the Lewis and Clark Expedition visited or camped in each of these three north Oregon coastal towns. The expedition set up camp for the winter at Fort Clatsop, just southwest of Astoria along the banks of the Lewis and Clark River. They were desperately in need of salt to cure and preserve meat in preparation for a long winter and return journey home. A group of five men set-off south towards present day Seaside, in search of an oceanside location for salt making. They eventually set up camp 15 miles south of Fort Clatsop, near the mouth of the Necanicum River at the location of present day Seaside.

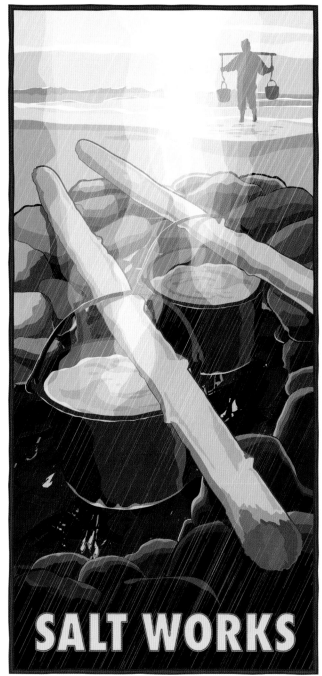

SALT WORKS

Game was plentiful in the area and salt was easily procured at a cairn they built close to the Pacific shore. In February of 1806, Captain Lewis and a group including Sacajawea stopped by the salt-making camp en route to modern day Cannon Beach in search of a beached whale. The cairn was closed soon after and the group returned to Fort Clatsop. Today, the site is preserved as a monument in Seaside, commemorating the westernmost encampment of the Lewis and Clark expedition.

Settlement in Seaside and the surrounding region really began as an offshoot of expansion south from the important port city of Astoria. The first official recorded settlement in Seaside was by a Mrs. Lattie and her children William and Helen when they purchased land in 1852 and 1853. The land claim covered 6,112 acres, including much of current downtown Seaside and all the way out to Tillamook Head. On this land, the family established the first boarding house in the Seaside area. The cooking of Helen Lattie soon became famous. For many years called "Lattie's", the business then became "The Summer House" in the late 1850's. It also later became the first postal designation for the community. Visitors to this first coastal retreat were in for an interesting experience by our modern standards. They came from Astoria and as far away as Portland by foot or horse down the beach, or by mail stage from the Skipanon Boat Landing near present day Warrenton.

Seaside's first major step in the direction of development began when a Portland land developer and railroad builder, Ben Holladay, visited the Summer House for the first time in 1870. He already had investments north near the Columbia River and became interested in the coastal area of Seaside following this visit. He soon purchased the Lattie's Summer House and began construction of his own property to be called the Seaside House. It was a large, classy wood-built resort that catered to wealthy visitors. On grounds were horse stables, a race-track, lawns and trees, and a stream running through. The resort would help classify Seaside at the time as an upscale coastal destination.

Holladay's Seaside House brought more visitors to the coast than ever before, with numbers at their peak reaching 350 – 400 during the busiest summer. Lack of transportation from Portland and abroad was a recurring complaint during this time.

Numerous attempts were made between 1853 and 1898 to finance and establish a quality railroad line from Portland to the coast. A large section of Holladay's business involved development and building of railroads, and he actually attempted to finance a line from Portland to Astoria. Unfortunately, he was not in a position financially to finish the project and it never got off the ground. By 1875, his wealth had crumbled and bankruptcy soon followed.

Progress, however, would not be thwarted by Holladay's financial collapse. The first public local railroad line was completed in 1890. It serviced an area from Young's Bay to Warrenton south to Seaside. A group of Astoria's citizens, with the help of early area developer A.B. Hammond, arranged for the first railroad from Portland to Astoria to be built in 1898. Hammond also eventually bought the small local railroad, extended it into Astoria and integrated it into the Portland line.

MAIN STREET. BURNED MAY 14TH. 1912.
SEASIDE. ORE.

With a solid transportation infrastructure now in place connecting the southern Clatsop coastal communities with Astoria, and Astoria with Portland, growth was soon to follow. The railroad brought new settlers, businesses and scores of new visitors to Seaside. As the century turned, the resident population had grown significantly. The Necanicum River, which runs parallel to the Pacific through town, separated what was at the time Seaside and West Seaside. Seaside was incorporated in 1899, followed by West Seaside in 1905.

In response to the growing number of summer visitors arriving by railroad, the city continued to develop. In 1905, Seaside's first newspaper, The Seaside Signal, was established by R.N. Watson. Outspoken and opinionated, Watson soon began pushing for new businesses to be established, a bank, and road construction. By 1910, the population between both Seaside and West Seaside numbered approximately 1,600, with a summer population increasing to nearly five times that amount.

Tragedy struck the Seaside area twice between 1910 and 1912. One of the community's largest local employers, The Seaside Lumber and Manufacturing Company, went bankrupt in 1910. The local bank shutdown as a result. This event hit the community hard economically. To make matters worse, a raging fire struck in 1912, destroying many businesses in Seaside east of the Necanicum River. Most members of the community responded to help the local volunteer fire department, and a brigade was sent from Astoria in an attempt to quell the damage.

The tragedy would not stop Seaside from rebuilding with a greater sense of purpose. In response to an ever increasing desire by its citizens, the two Seaside communities east and west of the river legally merged in 1913. New organizations and developments were soon to take root. The Seaside Signal's new owner and publisher, E.N. Hurd, formed the Breakwater Association, which later became the Chamber of Commerce. The Seaside Women's Club was formed in 1913, and through their influence over the next 20 years, the city library was improved in 1919, mail was delivered to homes in 1935, and the first Dahlia Show occurred in 1931. Seaside's first high school was officially constructed in 1916, and plans were made to build Seaside's famous Promenade along the Pacific shore.

Following World War I and a brief hiatus from activity, Seaside again set its sites toward improvement and growth. Roads were built, hotels sprung up along the beach, business set up shop in town and the Promenade, with its famous downtown turnaround, was officially finished in 1920. Visitors from abroad still reached Seaside by train, but with the growing popularity of the automobile, it was time for some much needed road construction.

Two major road projects would change the face of travel to the area forever. The great north – south coastal highway called The Oregon Coastal Highway, or Highway 101, was commissioned by President Roosevelt in 1926. This highway was built to start in Astoria and passes directly through Seaside. Sunset Highway, connecting Portland with the coast, was completed in 1938, reducing the distance to less than 100 miles.

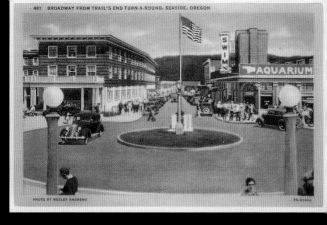

Seaside experienced the Great Depression much like the rest of the country. By 1940, the post-depression economy began to improve. A new sewage system was constructed, more roads were paved, and a jail was built. Buildings sprang up and bridges across the Necanicum River connected east and west Seaside at more locations. The economy again hit a snag with the explosion of WWII. Following the war, tourism would be the dominant force behind the continued growth of the community. Seaside made a concerted effort to promote its beach destination around the northwest.

Today, the community of Seaside is a unique tourist destination set alongside one of the most beautiful beaches in the state of Oregon. The years following WW II were marked by growth, fueled by the continuing development of a rich tourist economy. This trend continues today. In many ways, the downtown Broadway corridor remains unchanged with the exception of a few newer buildings and some recent aesthetic changes to existing structure. Shops and businesses, new and old, cater to the rush of visitors during the busy months. Seaside will continue to be a desired coastal destination for years to come.

13 THE ENGAGEMENT RING SEASIDE PARK.

Seaside, Oregon

Greetings from Seaside Oregon

SEASIDE

Art & Atmosphere

LOCATED HALFWAY BETWEEN ARTSY Cannon Beach to the south, and historical Astoria to the north along the Columbia River, is the community of Seaside. Seaside has always maintained its own unique identity, with a history of quaint beach cottages, carousels and roller coasters, salt-water taffy and elephant ears. It has been known and loved for its family atmosphere, with an abundance of restaurants, shopping and recreational activities. Seaside sits along one of the northwest's most beautiful beaches, with majestic Tillamook Head watching over it from the south and offering protection for "The Cove," a favorite surfing spot.

The downtown corridor is reminiscent of an east coast beach town, with the promenade, arcade, taffy shops, restaurants and hotels just steps from the ocean. Seaside has long been a favored family vacation destination, drawing visitors on the train from Portland in the early days, and today by vehicle from the northwest and beyond. Though much has changed over the years, Seaside's family charm remains the same. Many of the original buildings still stand and the festive atmosphere is consistent year after year, especially during the busiest times like summer and

Seaside

where the stars play!

DILLON © 1997

D. Carmicheal Courtesy of Seaside Chamber of Commerce   G. Vetter

T. Robinson   M. Larson

THE IDENTITY OF A COASTAL TOWN

Since its early beginnings, Seaside has always been a coastal community built on visitor traffic and tourism. From Ben Holladay's first upscale destination, the Summer House, to the shops and tourist attractions lining Broadway today, to the new condominium development on the promenade, the economic lifeblood of this unique coastal community pumps in time with the changing seasons.

Downtown Seaside has at times been likened to famous east coast beach resorts like Coney Island, with its arcade, souvenir shops, restaurants, bumper cars, and oceanfront promenade. Like most coastal destinations, visitor traffic is largely contingent upon weather and the seasons. However, unlike many Oregon coastal resorts, Seaside boasts a wide diversity of visitors, from hipster teenagers to families, and most other known demographics in between.

D. Masterson

D. Masterson

D. Masterson

D. Masterson

BUMPER CAR

RIDES 15¢

When Spring Breaks hit northwest schools and universities in March and April, Seaside is flooded with hot cars and young people looking for a good time. Seaside has long been one of the northwest's premier Spring Break destinations. In the past, it was not for those desiring quiet and beach solitude. Over the years, some crazy and interesting things have occurred, including a lifeguard tower rolling down Broadway and near riots on the streets. The city has worked hard to control the Spring Break chaos and make the atmosphere family friendly, but some locals still wonder if MTV may show up some year.

During the summertime, the atmosphere in Seaside is very family-oriented. Couples, families and children stroll the downtown, beaches and promenade, enjoying the laid back pace of beach life. Summer and fall are also times that bring the widest diversity of visitors, including retirees, international visitors and many more.

Many of Seaside's original downtown buildings have received face-lifts during the past few years, reflecting the sustained viability of the community as a favored coastal getaway. With the changes, it has still managed to maintain its original uniqueness and flair, with many of the classic elements still present, including the promenade, arcade and bumper cars, an elephant ear shop, and of course the aquarium. All of these are the legacy of a town that has never really struggled with its identity.

M. Larson

G. Vetter

T. Robinson

D. Masterson

Jennifer Lake Miller

D. Frank

FOR FRIED CLAMS

Separate clams carefully, then bread and fry in piping hot pan. Be cautious not to fry clams too long, which will toughen them. One minute on each side will leave clams tender.

Clams may also be served cold as appetizers. Heat liquid for hot broth or add milk for soup.

NOTICE

In order to retain the original iodine content these clams have not been bleached and on this account may be of a more or less brown color.

Contents 9 to 12 clams
Net Weight 19 oz.

First *Quality*

PACKED BY
SEASIDE CLAM CO.
SEASIDE, OREGON
U. S. A.

Seaside

BRAND

NEW TENDERIZED

WHOLE

RAZOR CLAMS

FOR FRYING

D. Masterson

SEASIDE CUISINE

Seaside has long had a diverse and interesting mix of dining options to choose from. Restaurants have come and gone over the years, but a few locally owned and operated favorites have now become icons. Dooger's Seafood and Grill, in the middle of downtown on Broadway, has long been serving fresh seafood, famous clam chowder, sandwiches, burgers, steaks and beer to locals and visitors alike. The Pig N' Pancake is also a mainstay, serving both breakfast and lunch, but best known for its pancakes, omelets and waffles. Sam's Seaside Café in downtown Seaside serves customers fresh fish & chips, burgers, sandwiches, salads, clam chowder, microbrews and more. Norma's ocean diner, another Seaside favorite, has been serving all varieties of fresh seafood since 1976, along with world renowned clam chowder. Vista Sea Café has welcomed visitors from its corner location for years.

If you happen to be in the mood for something other than seafood, Seaside has something to meet every dining need. Fultano's Pizza and the Pizza Harbor, both located in the downtown area, as well as the Creekside Pizzeria along the Neawanna River, can fulfill your craving for Italian. Another favorite restaurant is the Bigfoot Pub & Grill, with its giant statue of Bigfoot the Sasquatch, staring out from the parking lot at passing cars. The historic Gilbert District, where Holladay and Broadway intersect, hosts Lil' Bayou, which offers down-home Cajun cooking at its best. The menu features appetizers, entrees, and desserts. The restaurant has become a local and visitor favorite, with its unique southern atmosphere, Cajun spice, and world-class menu options.

ZUCCINI SEAFOOD BOAT

Serves 2

INGREDIENTS

Combine following spices in small bowl:

1 tsp. paprika

1 tsp. salt

1/4 tsp. cayenne pepper

1/4 tsp. white pepper

1/4 tsp. black pepper

1/2 tsp. granulated garlic

1/2 tsp. granulated onion

1/2 tsp. oregano

1/2 tsp. thyme

1/2 tsp. basil

2 large zucchini

4 large shrimp

1 and 1/2 cup small shrimp

1 and 1/2 cup crawfish tail meat

4 scallions

3 whole artichoke hearts, quartered

1/4 cup sherry

1/4 cup white wine

1 and 1/2 cup oil, reserving 2 tsp. oil

1 and 1/2 cup flour

4 eggs, mixed with 1 1/2 cup milk

1 1/2 cup Panko crumbs

METHOD

Cut zucchinis in half lengthwise. With the tip of a tablespoon, scoop out the pulp and set aside. Dredge hollow zucchini halves in egg wash, then flour mixture. Dip in egg wash once again, then coat with Panko crumbs. Heat oil in heavy skillet over medium heat. Pan-fry coated zucchini until Panko crumbs brown.

In separate skillet, heat reserved 2 tsp. oil over medium-high heat. Add seafood, artichoke hearts, and zucchini filling. Sprinkle with 1 tsp. of spice mixture. Cook until color starts to show on shrimp. Sprinkle with 1 tbsp. flour and toss. Add sherry and white wine. Simmer until thickened. Fill the zucchini boats with seafood mixture. Place boats on baking sheet, finish cooking in 400 degree oven for five minutes. Serve with mashed potatoes.

O. Masterson

D. Masterson

LIL' BAYOU SALMON FILLETS

Serves 2

INGREDIENTS

Spice Mixture:

1 tsp. paprika

1 tsp. salt

1/4 tsp. cayenne pepper

1/4 tsp. white pepper

1/4 tsp. black pepper

1/2 tsp. granulated onion

1/2 tsp. oregano

1/2 tsp. thyme

1/2 tsp. basil

2 seven oz. salmon filets

4 tbsp. canola oil

Sauce:

1 cup Merlot

1 tsp. corn starch

3 Tablespoons cola

METHOD

Coat filets lightly with oil and sprinkle both sides lightly with spice. In a non-stick pan, sauté' over medium high heat for 2 minutes on each side. Finish cooking filets in 400 degree oven for 5 - 7 minutes. Meanwhile, simmer Merlot on medium-high heat until it is reduced by half. Mix cola and cornstarch together, pour slowly into hot Merlot and stir until thickened. Serve Merlot reduction sauce over filets.

CHOCOLATE-BANANA BREAD PUDDING

INGREDIENTS

4 large eggs, lightly beaten

1 cup brown sugar

3 cups cream

1 cup milk

1 tsp. vanilla extract

3/4 tsp. cinnamon

3 ripe, mashed bananas

8 cups half-inch dice day old French bread

8 oz. semi sweet chocolate chips

Whipped cream, for garnish

METHOD

Preheat oven to 350 degrees. Spray 10 X 14 inch baking pan with cooking spray.

In large bowl, whisk together eggs, brown sugar, cream and milk. Stir in vanilla, cinnamon, bananas, bread and chocolate chips. Let mixture sit for 5 minutes in bowl, stir, and then transfer to baking dish. Bake on middle rack for 1 hour, until just set. Garnish with whipped cream. Refrigerate leftovers.

D. Masterson

T. Robinson

G. Vetter

G. Vetter

T. Robinson

B. Jenson

T. Robinson

M. Larson

D. Bartholet

A DAY AT THE BEACH

The stretch of Oregon Coast along Highway 101 through Cannon Beach, Seaside and Astoria is an outdoor lover's dream, with its many accessible beaches, rivers, bays, and of course the Pacific Ocean. Visitors to Seaside don't have to look too far for entertainment. Downtown offers shopping, dining, an arcade, bumper cars, miniature golf and much more. During the summertime, the community hosts a variety of special events including the Annual Beach Volleyball Tournament and the Fourth of July celebration. For those wishing to venture beyond downtown and experience the area's rich recreational offerings, all you need is a little information and the right equipment.

At the far south end of the beach, the ocean carves in against the back-drop of Tillamook Head at an area known as "the cove". Surfers favor the waves that wrap around the promentory and break not far off shore. This area is not for beginning surfers however, with its giant boulders exposed at low tide and strong rip-currents along the south point.

The cove is also a great spot for ocean fishing from the sand or off the rocks. But use caution and be aware of sneaker waves, slippery rocks and rolling logs. When the tides are low enough, razor clam diggers hit the beach with waders or boots, shovels, and clam guns. This activity is always dependent upon the tides, which don't always occur during the day. When low tide falls at night, clam diggers bring lanterns or flashlights for a late night dig.

M. Vargas

M. Larson

D. Beeston

D. Frank

D. Frank

Spectacular crabbing and salmon fishing can be found within the city limits, from Avenue U to 12th Avenue along the Necanicum River. Both can be done from one of Seaside's many bridges, or an avid fisherman can find a spot along the river bank. If you have access to a boat, the estuary at the mouth of the river is a perfect spot as well. Be sure to consult local regulations for necessary licensing requirements, catch and size limits. Taking responsibility for sustaining clam, crab and fish populations for future generations is a crucial part of the local outdoor recreation experience.

The area also offers a variety of non-harvesting outdoor activities. Tillamook Head is a perfect spot for hiking or mountain biking the Oregon Coast Trail, located just past the cove on the south end of town. Wildlife enthusiasts can witness gray whale migration in the spring, or possibly catch site of eagles, falcons and many other species of birds. Other area activities include biking or skating along the promenade, golfing on one of many nearby courses, testing your hand or feet with the paddle boats downtown, stunt kite flying on the beach, or kayaking the river. Recreational pursuits are never far away during a visit to Seaside. Something exciting and new is always just around the corner for every type of visitor.

SEASIDE EVENTS

Much like neighboring cities Cannon Beach and Astoria, the planned event in Seaside has become a key component in bringing visitors to town and entertaining the local population. Events take place throughout the year, although the largest, most popular occur during the summer months.

The holiday season brings the annual gift fair, an event highlighting artisans and gift proprietors at the Seaside Civic & Convention Center. It is a great opportunity to get needed Christmas shopping done. Another holiday season event is the Parade of Lights. Participants travel the streets of Seaside, with a dash of holiday caroling thrown in to make things interesting.

Seaside's Independence Day – Fourth of July celebration kicks off the summer season with music, a street fair, and a stunning firework display in the evening. Visitors flock to the beach for this celebration each year. Fireworks are lit throughout the afternoon and evening, culminating with the community's own stunning, professionally supervised firework display.

The Hood-to-Coast Relay and Annual Beach Volleyball Tournament in August have grown to mammoth proportions, drawing participants and spectators from across the United States and around the world. The Hood-to-Coast Relay is thought to be the world's largest relay race, stretching 197 miles from atop Mount Hood and through Portland, to finish beside the Pacific Ocean in Seaside. Teams assemble and travel from around the world to take place in this event. Competitors are greeted at the finish line in Seaside with festivities, food and music.

D. Carmicheal Courtesy of Seaside Chamber of Commerce

The Annual Beach Volleyball Tournament is the largest amateur participation tournament in the country, taking place each year in August. Teams compete in a variety of categories, ranging from 14 and under to 45 and over. Throughout the weekend, the beach in front of the turnaround is like a carnival; highlighted with product give-aways and sampling, food booths, merchandise vendors, music and a live DJ.

M. Larson

T. Robinson

D. Frank

M. Larson

D. Frank

B. Jenson

Seaside:
where the
stars play

RIDE THE STREETCAR!

T. Robinson

CANNON BEAC

History

THE HISTORY OF CANNON BEACH is a tale of fierce independence, hardy settlers, lost and found cannons, visionaries and brave individualists. It is fitting then, that the first non-native American people to visit the Cannon Beach area were members of the Lewis and Clark expedition. They were a rugged group of trailblazers ending a journey across the untouched landscape of our country. Their first glimpse of the Cannon Beach shores occurred in January of 1806. Captain William Clark, upon cresting Tillamook Head caught his first glimpse of the Pacific shore and exclaimed:

"From this point I beheld the grandest and most pleasing prospect which my eyes ever surveyed."

The expedition was in search of a beached whale nearby, the carcass of which contained valuable blubber and oil. It was here they also had a friendly encounter with the native Tillamook Indians. After finding the whale, they returned to their encampment at Fort Clatsop near Astoria. This was to be the last we hear of the Cannon Beach area for several decades.

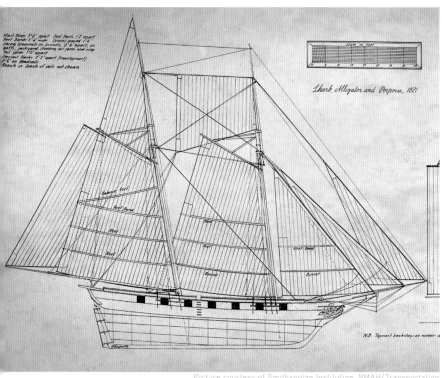

Picture courtesy of Smithsonian Institution, NMAH/Transportation

In 1846, the United States Navy schooner, Shark, sank while attempting to cross the Columbia Bar near Astoria. Wreckage from the ship including three cannons washed ashore near Hug Point, just south of Cannon Beach. Some accounts claim that a party of Indians and a U.S. Midshipman removed the cannons to a nearby creek-bed for safekeeping and named the area Cannon Beach. Due to weather and over time, the cannons were eventually lost from memory.

In the early days on the coast, a single man (or woman) generally carried coastal mail from point to point on a horse. On one such route, mail carrier, Bill Luce, discovered one of the lost cannons. It was removed to sit in front of the Austin House, an early traveler's lodge, and eventually ended up in the hotel's barn. Ironically, the name, Cannon Beach, remained in this area, though it is actually modern day Arch Cape.

90

In 1890, the first railroad was built between Young's Bay in Astoria and the coastal town of Seaside. Previously, travelers to the area had to endure a boat ride down the Columbia River from Portland, followed by a miserable stagecoach ride to Seaside. As coastal travel became easier, many began to set their sights further southward to Cannon Beach.

Subsequently, a toll-road was built following an old Indian trail through the forest from Seaside to Elk Creek. The area would become what is now Cannon Beach. Travel from Elk Creek to Seaside and beyond was by necessity only, perhaps to visit a doctor, or to acquire staples such as flour, sugar, salt, and oil. Traveling by car today, the trip takes approximately 10 minutes. Not so for the early settlers. It was usually an all-day event through rivers and forests.

In 1892, a sawmill proprietor by the name of Herbert Logan built the first hostelry within the boundaries of the Elk Creek/Cannon Beach area. The 16-room Logan House, later known as the Elk Creek Hotel, sat on the north side of Ecola Creek roughly where the Ecola Creek Lodge is located today. With a place to now lay their heads, visitors began to frequent this formerly remote location.

Before 1910, road access in and out of Ecola was difficult at best. In the years following the establishment of a post office, several major road improvements were completed in the area. Because vehicles were allowed to drive the beaches, at this time a road was blasted around the rock wall at Hug Point south of Ecola, an area previously impassible except during the lowest tides. The road from Seaside to Ecola was improved, reducing north/south travel time to a mere 30 minutes. Locally, a bridge was built over the creek on the north end, eliminating a previously unreliable ferry crossing.

In 1910, at the bequest of Elk Creek's residents and summer visitors, a petition was made to Washington, D.C. for a Post Office to be established in the community. It was soon approved. The area was given an official title, "Ecola", by the United States Government. Accordingly, the village of Elk Creek, now Ecola, was finally given formal recognition. It was during the early part of the 19th century that infrastructure development really began in the area.

D. Masterson Courtesy of Martin Hospitality

In 1912 the first water system was built to service twelve customers in the presidential street area. Three years later a telephone system was installed, with 10 shared party lines. Although Ecola boasted fewer than 100 full-time residents at this time, it was a step in the direction of progress!

A logging camp and mill were established around 1912, and more people began to settle in the following years. Relocation and settlement meant more children and a subsequent need for a central school. The first school classes were conducted in a local hotel before being moved to a rented house. In 1921 a one-room schoolhouse was built specifically for educational purposes, but was often used for church services as well.

In 1922, the citizens of Ecola petitioned for a community name change. Postal confusions with a similarly named Willamette Valley town were common enough to warrant changing the town's name. In a vote, the citizens of Ecola decided to adopt the name Cannon Beach, now abandoned by the community of Arch Cape, just a few miles south where the original cannon had been found.

During the years following, Cannon Beach continued to modernize; adopting new roads, plumbing, electricity, weekend homes and a more organized community structure. Hotels and traveler's stops became more and more frequent and consequently visitor traffic increased.

Post World War II marked an era of significant growth in our country, and Cannon Beach was no exception. The town took care of some much needed improvements by installing asphalt sidewalks to replace what were a series of unreliable wooden boardwalks. A commercial club (Boosters) was formed to provide for the town's basic needs, and a fire department was created after a house burned to the ground. New businesses, buildings, and streets sprang up everywhere. The population increased and utility improvements continued. In 1950, the Sunset Highway was completed between Portland and the coast, reducing travel time to an hour and a half.

Infrastructure growth encouraged more visitors, but to some residents the increase in tourism meant unwanted changes. To many, it seemed that community incorporation was a necessary step, others desired to maintain the same sleepy, relatively unknown atmosphere. After much local debate and controversy, Cannon Beach was finally officially incorporated in 1955.

According to one prominent local resident, the current state and character of Cannon Beach would not have been possible without the efforts of two early visionaries; Maurie Clark and Ray Watkins. In the early 1960's, the town showed signs of age and dilapidation. Fueled by Watkins aesthetic creativity and Clark's philanthropy, a variety of building projects were undertaken. Examples include the Coaster Theater, Mariner Market, the library, and the Chamber of Commerce building. The result of their work enhanced and beautified Cannon Beach. Their attitude proved to be contagious. Residential districts were improved in the spirit of change, and over time, a marked transformation was completed within the community.

This transformation spurred other changes in the character and identity of the community. Cannon Beach would become an art community; not really a surprise, considering the beauty of the natural surroundings. Tourism would continue to flourish, soon becoming the primary commercial industry. Cannon Beach was becoming what it is today - an economy built on tourism and travel, a place to retire, and one of the most beautiful towns on the Oregon Coast.

471 HUG POINT, CANNON BEACH, OREGON

HAYSTACK ROCK

PHOTO BY WESLEY ANDREWS

8A-H3205

Wildlife
of
Haystack
Rock

Cannon
Beach,
Oregon

CANNON
BEACH
SO WONDERFULLY
Different

n Beach

fully Different!

H Art & Atmosphere

TUCKED AWAY BETWEEN MOUNTAINS and the sea, Cannon Beach is a true paradise and people are drawn to this unique Oregon coast community for many reasons. The area's stunning beauty cannot be matched. For years, photographers and artists have found Cannon Beach a natural fit; a place of inspiration and magic.

What began as a remote beach settlement and logging community has today become one of the Northwest's most vibrant and popular art scenes. Each year Cannon Beach hosts two events, Spring Unveiling in May and The Stormy Weather Arts Festival in November. Both are celebrations of art, photography, music and cuisine; a gathering of those who capture and connect with the beauty of Cannon Beach. In this chapter, we hope to celebrate these mediums as well.

T. Robinson

TierneyHull

J. Hull

D. Frank

D. Masterson

K. Nyberg

D. Masterson

1042. HAIR PIN BEND ON BOULEVARD, SEA SIDE TO CANNON BEACH, OREGON.

EARLY TRAVELS

Cannon Beach visitors today sure have it easy. Gone are the days of long train journeys, boat trips, ferry crossings, and stage coach rides down rudimentary roads. When the sun is shining, a day trip to the beach and back to the city is a rather common affair. Due to geographic isolation or public sentiment, Cannon Beach has always seemed to exist a little farther down the beaten trail than its neighbors Seaside and Astoria. For many years, a Cannon Beach trip was more of an adventure than the mellow car ride we are now accustomed to.

In 1933, Coastal Highway 101 was completed from Canada to Mexico. The great highway originally passed directly through Cannon Beach along the way, but was eventually moved to its current location outside of town. Before the highway's completion, motorists traveling from the south were forced to drive on the beach to reach their destinations. This usually meant time spent waiting for rudimentary ferries to allow crossing of coastal rivers, and an awareness of changing tides to allow passage around certain outcropping rocky points. One of the most famous tidal-passages was located at Hug Point, that vast outcropping located a few miles south of Cannon Beach. A rudimentary road was eventually blasted into the rock and can still be seen today.

D. Masterson

The majority of Cannon Beach day-trippers come from Portland and the Willamette Valley. Before 1941, the only way folks from the Portland area and north could reach Cannon Beach was along the Columbia River and down Highway 30 through Astoria. It was an excruciating journey of 5-6 hours from Portland alone. Once the Cannon Beach junction was reached, travelers were then faced with 111 curves leading into town. Talk about carsickness! Coastal family trips must have been a true test of patience for all involved.

T. Robinson

D. Masterson

K. Nyberg

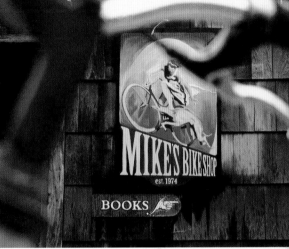

D. Masterson

D. Masterson

D. Masterson

K. Nyberg

G. Moon

G. Moon

T. Robinson

D. Masterson

T. Robinson

B. Steidel

D. Masterson

D. Masterson

CANNON BEACH CUISINE

For most visitors, one of the highlights of a Cannon Beach vacation is a meal at that favorite dining destination. Here you will find a variety of breakfast, lunch or dinner options; catering to couples, friends and families alike. Whether its pancakes at the Pig N' Pancake, an omelet at The Lazy Susan, a burger and beer at the Warren House, or wine and seafood at Newman's at 988; the options are as varied as people who visit Cannon Beach.

Enjoy a seat on the oceanfront and clam chowder at Oregon icon, Mo's restaurant, south of town in the Tolovana area. A lunch of fresh fish and chips or chowder at Ecola Seafood downtown is not to be missed. If you prefer Italian at the beach, Pizza A' Fetta and Fultano's in the middle of downtown, offer pizza, salads, soup, sandwiches and microbrews. For dinner, make your way to the north end of downtown for dinner at the quaint, classy restaurant, The Bistro. Or cross the street to JP's, and watch the chef create your meal from the dining room. Later in the evening, head down to The Wayfarer Restaurant in midtown for a nightcap and a delectable dessert or arrive earlier to enjoy a sunset with a magnificent view of Haystack Rock while you dine.

Located in an old house, on the south end of mid-town, French-Italian eatery Newman's at 988 is one of Cannon Beach's finest. Renowned Chef John Newman and wife Sandy bring a unique dining option to the Cannon Beach area. High quality appetizers, delectable entrees, complimentary wines and desserts are served from 5:30 – 9:00 in the cozy but elegant dining room. Reservations are highly recommended, and upon arrival, owner Sandy Newman will often greet you. The friendly and professional staff is there to meet your every need. An evening with the Newman's and their staff feels like a world class dining experience in the comfort of home.

D. Frank

D. Masterson

LOBSTER RAVIOLI

Makes 4 pc. ravioli

INGREDIENTS

Ravioli

8 pc. wonton skins (you can get these at your local store)

2 oz. cooked lobster meat

1/2 tsp. lemon juice

White fish mousse 2oz.

1 oz. white fish: halibut, ling cod etc.

1.5 oz. cream

1/2 tsp. lemon juice

1 tsp. chop parsley

S&P

1/2 tsp. toasted chopped hazelnuts

Sauce

1 oz. butter

1 tbsp. chop shallots

2 oz. sweet marsala wine

1 oz. cream

1/2 tsp. lemon juice

S&P

D. Masterson

METHOD

Fish mousse: Make the fish mousse in a robocoup by putting all the ingredients for the fish mousse in together and mixing until light and fluffy.

Toast the hazelnuts in the oven until golden brown. Set aside.

Ravioli: Place 1/2 oz. cooked lobster & 1/2 oz. fish mousse in middle of wonton skin, moisten the edges of the wonton skin with cold water, place another wonton skin on top and seal the ravioli. Repeat this process to get more raviolis.

Sauce: Sauté the shallots in the butter for 1 minute, add marsala and reduce by half, add cream and reduce by half. Add lemon, salt and pepper.

Cook the ravioli in boiling water for two minutes. Remove from water, place on plate, sauce the plate with the marsala sauce and finish with toasted hazelnuts.

PETRALE SOLE STUFFED WITH DUGEONESS CRAB

Serves 2

INGREDIENTS

2 ea. 5 oz sole fillets

2 oz. fresh Dungeness crab

6 oz. brown rice

4 oz. assorted seasonal vegetables

1 oz. chopped shallots

4 oz. white wine

3 oz. butter

1 tbsp. fresh lemon juice

Salt and pepper

1/4 oz. caviar

D. Masterson

METHOD

Petrale sole, rice & veggies: Season sole and place crab in center of fillet and role into a roulade shape (round shape). Heat 1/2 oz. oil in sauté pan and sear sole golden brown, turn fillet over and finish cooking by roasting in 350 degree oven until cooked. Cook rice and vegetables to your liking.

Butter sauce: Reduce wine and shallots in a sauce pan until almost dry. Stir in butter, lemon, salt and pepper.

Finish the dish by placing your favorite caviar on top of the fish. Serve and enjoy!

WHOLE WHEAT GNOCCI

Serves 2 appetizer size portions

INGREDIENTS

4 oz. ricotta cheese

1 oz. grated parmesan

1 tsp. chopped parsley

1 tbsp. whole wheat flour

2 tbsp. ap flour

Eggplant

1 ea. eggplant

1 ea. shallot chopped

1/2 ea. leeks (cleaned & large diced)

1 tsp. saracha

1 tsp. honey

D. Masterson

METHOD

Mix ingredients together and set aside. Roast eggplant in the oven until tender. Sauté shallot and leeks until tender. Combine all ingredients together in robocoup, mix well and season with S & P.

Carrots: Cut carrots on a Japanese vegetable slicer and heat in a sauté pan with S&P.

Parmesan Crisp: Grate 2 tbsp. parmesan and heat in non stick pan until golden brown.

Carrot sauce: Juice 1 ea carrot. Reduce juice on stove until syrupy.

JEFFREY Hull

C. Bryant

R. Gorsuch

G. Schmidt

THE MAGIC OF ECOLA STATE PARK

Ecola State Park, located two miles out of town on Cannon Beach's north end is thought to be one of the most photographed spots in the world. With its elevated, panoramic views of Cannon Beach, the Pacific Ocean, Tillamook Rock Lighthouse, and Tillamook Head to the north; it is little wonder that photographers and artists are drawn to the park from around the world.

The Lewis and Clark expedition passed through in 1806 on their way over Tillamook Head in search of whale blubber near Ecola creek in Cannon Beach. It is near here that William Clark wrote famously in his journal: "From this point I beheld the grandest and most pleasing prospect which my eyes ever surveyed." What a description from a man who had witnessed the vast splendor of the Rocky Mountains and numerous other breathtaking sights on the expedition across the country. Visitors today are blessed with the same vantage point, carefully preserved as a National Park.

It wasn't until 1932 however, that Ecola State Park was officially classified as such; thanks to a generous land donation from a collection of early Cannon Beach families to the state of Oregon. Two-hundred twenty-five acres were either given freely or sold to the state to allow it to be preserved as a local highlight and visitor destination. One hundred and twelve acres were later added in 1948.

T. Robinson

ECOLA
— STATE PARK —

G. Moon

Over the years, the park has also served as a Hollywood destination for several notable films. "Kindergarten Cop" starring Arnold Schwarzenegger had a carnival scene filmed in 1993. The movie "Point Break", starring Keanu Reeves and Patrick Swayze brought film crews to Indian Beach just north of the park in 1996 for a memorable surf-fight scene. The classic 1985 hit, "The Goonies" also had several scenes filmed around the park and along the road leading in.

Ecola State Park, with its views, stunning scenery, and unique history, has served as host for decades of memories. It sits majestic and preserved, like a sentinel watching over Cannon Beach and the Pacific Ocean. All travelers to this section of the Oregon Coast should make the park a destination for photographs and memories yet to come.

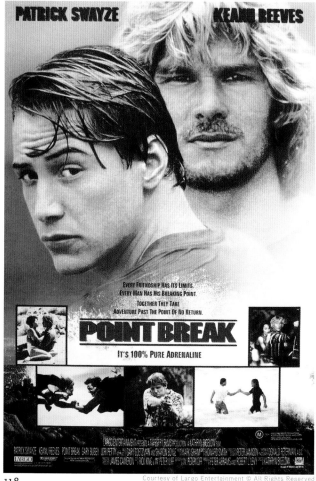

B. Jenson

T. Robinson

T. Robinson

T. Robinson

CANNON BEACH EVENTS

Tourist communities like Cannon Beach often measure the changing seasons by weather, visitor traffic and key seasonal events. Throughout the year, Cannon Beach hosts a series of events catering to hearty winter art lovers in November, serious art appreciators in May, Sandcastle experts in June, and summer families in July. Each event caters to a different crowd and reveals the diversity and loyalty of Cannon Beach's many visitors.

The Stormy Weather Arts Festival celebrates the richness of Cannon Beach's local art scene. It falls on the first weekend in November, and as the name implies, weather is often as unpredictable as the sea itself. Stormy or clear, visitors come prepared with winter clothes and a positive attitude for a wonderful weekend of art, food, events and people. In the afternoons and evenings, visitors can walk the town and enjoy live music, gallery hosted displays replete with food and drink, and conversation with fellow art lovers. A highlight of the weekend is the Quick-Draw event, where artists represented in the community's galleries convene to demonstrate their prowess by creating a work of art in an hour. Each piece is displayed at the conclusion of the event and attendees bid, auction-style, on their favorite art.

'Twas the night before...

SANDCASTLE DAY

CANNON BEACH

The 42nd Annual Sandcastle Contest
June 17th 2006

© 2006 closerrider

D. Masterson

G. Vetter

D. Masterson

D. Pastor

G. Moon

T. Robinson

G. Moon

The Haystack Holidays at the beginning of December feature a series of events to officially kick off the holiday season. Highlights include wreath making, a lamp-lighting ceremony downtown, and an event for children to enjoy craft making, cookie decoration, refreshments and Santa Claus. Christmas Eve through New Years is one of the few winter weeks that draw visitors to town again.

Spring Unveiling during the first weekend in May again caters to the community's art loving visitors. Artists and galleries unveil new pieces and host receptions all weekend long. This event kicks off a new season after the long winter for Cannon Beach's vibrant art scene.

D. Masterson

Cannon Beach's oldest and perhaps best known event, the annual Sandcastle Contest, takes place in June. Not much has changed in the 40+ years since the event's founding. Professionals and amateurs hit the beach when the tide is at its lowest; with sand tools and high expectations. A panel of judges votes on the best from each category of sandcastle building experience. Visitors soon follow to observe each creation, stroll along the shore, and enjoy a unique day at the beach.

The true summer season begins with celebrating our country's independence during the Fourth of July Weekend. Cannon Beach shuts down the streets in the morning for a colorful parade along Hemlock St. Participants include children on decorated bicycles, walking groups, and folks in vehicles throwing candy to observers lining the streets.

K. Nyberg

TREASURES ON THE BEACH

For generations of Cannon Beach locals and visitors, the Japanese glass float has embodied the pinnacle of beachcombing achievement. Light green, perfectly round, and existing in a wide variety of sizes, this delicate glass orb has long been considered the king's treasure. Wonder and mystery are at the heart of the quest for this elusive piece of flotsam. As many locals will attest, there is no rhyme or reason to the appearance of the Japanese glass float. Some will claim to have a grasp on the ideal weather, ocean currents, and tidal activity, but still the perfect glass float conditions remain largely a mystery.

At least twice in Cannon Beach's history, all these unknown elements have come together to create a perfect glass float day. One local remembers walking on the beach to school with a friend on a spring day, late 1960's. This day began much like any other, but soon became something both would remember vividly for the next forty years. What set it apart was the multitude of glass floats lining the shore. The girls claim to have found more than 24 that spring day, an unheard of amount even for a serious glass float hunter.

The following account, related by Peter Lindsay in "Comin Over the Rock: A Storyteller's History of Cannon Beach", describes the perfect conditions as told to him by a seasoned float hunter: "We need to get down just after high tide. Strong west winds, due west and blowing steadily, they're the best. When the Velella show up (a small blue jelly fish, related to the Portuguese Man O" War) that's a really good sign. Fish floats come in when the Vellela get blown onto the beach. I usually find them concentrated in pretty much the same places time after time: around Haystack Rock, near the mouth of Elk Creek, at the base of Chapman Point".

If the idea of a glass float from a distant shore intrigues you, give these destinations a shot. You might just find your own treasure on the beach.

T. Robinson

T. Robinson

S. Pastor

ACKNOWLEDGEMENTS

We would like to offer a special thank you to everyone who encouraged and supported us through this second project. It took a bit longer than we thought, but here we are with a book we are very proud of. First of all, we would like to thank our families: Jeff and Jean Carlsen, Don and Barb Masterson, Erin, Kyle, Grandma, Monica & Ehren and Andrea & Garth. You believe in us and our crazy ideas like no other. Our friends: Mark and Jenny Piscitelli and David and Molly Marshal. Ashleigh and Nalu for your understanding through the process. Thank you Melisa Kroening for once again helping make this possible. Thomas Robinson – Once again your talent has shown through. A very special "thank you" to Sarah and Chuck from The Compleat Photographer for all your help. We would also like to offer a special thank you to artists and photographers: Don Frank, Patrick Corcoran, George Vetter, Gary Moon, Rosetta Hurley, Noel Thomas, Chris Bryant, Bill Jensen, Bill Dodge, Mark Larson, David J. Carmicheal, Jeffery Hull, Richard Gorsuch, Geoff Schmidt, Dave and Suzie Pastor, Darren Orange, Jennifer Lake Miller, Sarah Goodnough, Bill Steidel, Dave Bartholet, Michael Mathis, Michelle Vargas, Mike Dillon, Carol Riley and Diane Beeston. Thank you also to Kim Bosse and the Cannon Beach Chamber of Commerce, Regina Willkie and the Astoria/Warrenton Chamber of Commerce, and Alan Smiles and the Seaside Chamber of Commerce. Jon and Sandy Newman – Thanks again for making things so easy. Thank you also to the Holen's at Baked Alaska and the Lil' Bayou Restaurant.

We would also like to thank: Kat Nyberg, Don Frank, The Nyberg family, Tina McBride, The Cannon Beach Historical Society, The Seaside Historical Society and Museum, Liisa Penner and The Clatsop County Historical Society, The Astoria Maritime Museum, Trendwest in Seaside, Jeff Womack, Valerie Ryan, The Good 'Ol Boy Club, Martin Hospitality, Sleepy Monk Coffee, David and Susie Pastor, Sailor Jerry, James Faurentino and Bella Espresso, Jon and Jan Knickerbocker, Bob and Glady Kaleta, David and Trina Robinson, Whitney Murphy, Paul van der Veldt, Mary Blake at Seaside Parks & Recreation, The Bald Eagle, The Dragonfire Gallery, The Elliot Hotel, Donna and The Cannery Pier Hotel, The staff at Fort Clatsop, The RiverSea Gallery, The National Parks Service, The Wet Dog Café, The Smithsonian Institution, Yale Collection of Western Americana, and the Beinecke Rare Book and Manuscript Library.

CREDITS

PHOTOGRAPHERS : Bryant, Chris : pp. 22, 23. Carmichael, David : pp. 63, 82. Corcoran, Patrick : pp 47, Cover Photo & Dust Jackets. Frank, Don : pp. 5, 23, 25, 32, 43, 70, 80, 83, 84, 101, 110, Cannon Beach & Seaside Dust Jackets. Hurley, Rosetta : pp. 37, 39, 41, 42. Jenson, Bill : pp. 78, 84, 118. Larson, Mark : pp. 5, 28, 40, 63, 67, 78, 80, 82, 85, 86. Masterson, Donald : pp. 1, 5, 6, 10, 19, 24, 25, 27, 28, 30, 31, 33, 34, 35, 37, 40, 44, 46, 60-61, 64, 67, 69, 72, 73, 74, 75, 93, 101, 103, 105, 108, 109, 110, 111, 112, 113, 121, 123, Dust Jackets. Mathis, Michael : pp. 28, Astoria Dust Jacket. Meyers, Chuck : pp 28. Moon, Gary : pp. 106, 107, 117, 122, 123, 126, Cover Photo & Dust Jackets. Nyberg, Kat : pp. 43, 101, 105, 123. Pastor, Dave : pp 121. Robinson, Thomas : pp. 7, 23, 38, 63, 65, 67, 76, 78, 83, 87, 98-99, 104, 108, 116, 119, 123, 124, Cannon Beach Dust Jacket. Vargas, Michelle : pp. 32, 44, 46, 80. Vetter, George : pp. 6, 23, 63, 67, 76, 77, 86, 121, Cover Photo & Dust Jackets. ARTISTS : Bartholet, Dave : pp 79. Beeston, Diane : pp. 30, 31, 43, 80. Bryant, Chris : pp 114. Dillon, Mike : pp 62. Dodge, Bill : pp 26. Goodnough, Sarah : pp. 36, 71. Gorsuch, Richard : pp 114. Hull, Jeffery : pp. 37, 100, 114, Dust Jackets. Masterson, Donald : pp. 5, 121. Miller, Jennifer Lake : pp 68. Myrah, Newman : pp 12. Orange, Darren : pp 39. Pastor, Suzie : pp 125. Riley, Carol : pp 86. Schmidt, Geoff : pp. 5, 115. Steidel, Bill : pp 109. Thomas, Noel : pp. 20-21, 29, 39, 42, Astoria Dust Jacket. HISTORICAL : The Alvena Nyberg Collection ; pp. 92, 94, 97. Cannon Beach Historical Society : pp. 120, 88, 89, 90, 92, 93, 94, 95. Clatsop County Historical Society : pp. 13, 14, 15, 16, 18, 19, 50, 51, 54, 55, 56, 91, 97. The Compleat Photographer : pp. 5, 14, 17, 18, 24, 95, 97, 102. The Knickerbocker Collection : pp. 5, 8-9, 14, 16, 48-49, 52, 53, 54-55, 56, 57, 58, 59, 92. Wesley Andrews : pp 57. Oregon State Capitol Legislative Administration Committee : pp 10. Independence National Historical Park Collection, National Park Service : pp 11. Mr. & Mrs. Harold Weston : pp 12. Smithsonian Institution : pp 90. Yale Collection of Western Americana, Beinecke Rare Book & Manuscript Library : pp 50 GENERAL : Largo Entertainment : pp 118. National Parks Service : pp. 40, 50, 116. Seaside Clam Co : pp 71, Seaside Dust Jacket. Union Fisherman's Co-operative Packing Co : pp 36. Universal City Studios : pp 45